The Startup

Choosing the Right

Legal Structure for Your Business

Sole Proprietorship
General Partnership
Limited Partnership
Limited Liability Partnership
Limited Liability Company
Subchapter S Corporation
C Corporation

Liability, Tax Treatment, and More

F. Lee Frye

Table of Contents

Chapter 1

The Importance of Choosing the

Right Business Structure

Of all the decisions you will make when starting a business, choosing the right business structure may be the most important. This decision will affect how much you pay in taxes, how much personal liability you face, as well as your ability to raise capital. It is not a decision that should be taken lightly and should be thoroughly researched before a decision is made.

The legal structures your business may choose are sole proprietorship, general partnership, limited partnership, limited liability partnership, limited liability company (LLC), subchapter S corporation, or a regular C corporation. When selecting which legal structure is best for your company you should consider several different criteria. These criteria involve legal liability, tax implications, cost of formation, ongoing costs, flexibility, and future needs.

Forms of Legal Business Structures	
Unincorporated Legal Structures	**Incorporated Legal Structures**
Sole Proprietorship	Limited Liability Company (LLC)
General Partnership	S Corporation
Limited Partnership	C Corporation
Limited Liability Partnership	

Legal liability for a business comes from two main sources, civil actions and contractual obligations. Civil actions or torts come from actions that the business has undertaken that has caused damage to others. This is not a criminal action because there was not intent for harm, yet damage or harm did occur. Examples of civil liability include a business with a faulty piece of equipment that causes someone to get hurt or a service that was rendered that was not completed properly. In either case, there was not intent to do harm, but the business can be held responsible for damage and incur hefty legal fees. Contractionary liability can occur when a loan goes into default or failing to compete the terms of a signed contract.

The first thought is that liability insurance can cover the costs of legal liability and in many cases it can. However, commercial general liability insurance only covers injury or property damage caused by the company and will not help with contractual liability. It is possible to add contractual liability insurance to your policy that will cover costs if the company fails to complete a contract, but will not help with default on debt. Additionally, some professions require specialized liability insurance such as malpractice insurance for doctors and lawyers. But insurance is not a catch all for every liability issue that may arise. There are exclusions to every insurance policy.

Exclusions are items that the insurance policy will not cover. Every insurance policy has a limit to coverage the policy will pay out. Therefore it is important to have enough insurance to cover expected losses. Also, unforeseen losses are not covered in most insurance policies. The bottom line is that insurance is not a perfect solution to all liability issues that a business may face.

When choosing a legal business structure an entrepreneur should also consider tax implications which can affect both business profits and their personal income. If you choose to remain unincorporated, all business profits will be claimed as personal income and will be taxed at the business owner's individual tax rate. By choosing a C Corporation business structure, business profits will be taxed at a corporate income tax rate. Once business profit has been taxed at the corporate tax rate, the owners (shareholders) can take distribution of the remaining income, which is paid in the form of a dividend. This dividend payment will then be taxed as individual income. The reality of the situation is that this income has been taxed two times. Once as profit from the corporation and then again as individual income. There is an alternative to double taxation by choosing a Limited Liability Company or S corporation as a business structure, also known as a "pass-through" entity. A "pass-through" entity does not tax income at the corporate level, all profits and losses are "passed-through" to the individual and the individual claims these profits and losses on their individual tax form to the IRS. However, a "pass-through" incorporated entity, requires the same extra paperwork of a C corporation that an unincorporated business does not have.

A third consideration when choosing the right legal structure for your business is the cost of formation. A sole proprietorship has virtually no costs associated with its legal structure; however partnerships may want agreements drawn up by attorneys, which would have additional costs. Corporations have even greater costs of formation due to registration requirements applicable to each state's corporation commission or secretary of state. Corporations not only have formation costs, but they have yearly renewal costs that must be considered.

A business also should consider flexibility and their future needs when choosing a legal business structure. Where is your business going? What are its long-term goals? These are important questions to answer prior to choosing your business' legal structure. Some types of legal structures will not allow for expansion and acquisitions. Do your long-term plans lead to an Initial Public Offering (IPO) of stocks? If so, you will need to set up your business as a C corporation. It is possible to change to a different type of structure after your business is operating, but there are timing issues, along with additional costs and paperwork.

There is one other consideration to make when choosing a business structure and that is continuation of existence of the business. If you want to secure your family's financial future, then you want to make sure your business can continue after you die or become incapacitated. Choosing the proper legal structure is important because a sole proprietorship dies with the business owner, other types of structures live on after the owner's demise.

Deciding on the right legal business structure for you company depends on many factors. Choosing incorrectly can affect your business' goals, as well as your personal and family goals. The wrong choice can also impact your wealth due to unforeseen liabilities. This book will look at each legal business structure and analyze each of the criteria mentioned above. Once you compare the choices of legal structures with your business's goals and your personal goals, it is possible to make the correct informed decision.

Chapter 2 in this book will focus on unincorporated legal business structures, while Chapter 3 will take on incorporated legal business structures. Unincorporated structures include sole proprietorships, general partnerships, limited partnerships and limited liability partnerships. Incorporated legal structures include limited liability company (LLC), S corporation, and C corporation. Chapter 4 details the steps required to form each type of business structure.

The two most important factors in deciding a legal business structure are liability and tax treatment. Chapter 5 explores types of liability that incorporating will not protect business owners from. Chapter 6 will discuss the tax treatment for each type of business structure, including the effects of the new Tax Cuts and Jobs Act of 2017 has on business structures.

Chapter 2

Unincorporated Legal Business Structures

A business can choose between two classes of business legal structures: incorporated and unincorporated. This chapter focuses on unincorporated structures which includes sole proprietorships, general partnerships, limited partnerships, and limited liability partnerships. Although businesses are regulated by state law and there are a few small differences regarding legal rights and obligations between some states, there are general characteristics and traits that unincorporated structures share. We will focus on the main differences of the criteria discussed in Chapter 1 which includes legal liability, tax implications, cost of formation, ongoing costs, flexibility, and future needs. We will also discuss the ability to transfer ownership and the continuity of the business after the owner's demise. See Appendix A for a quick reference guide for choosing a legal business structure.

Type of Structure	Number of Owners	Liability	Taxation
Sole Proprietorship	Only one owner.	Unlimited liability for owner.	Pass-Through All profits or losses taxed as an individual
General Partnership	More than one owner with no limits.	Unlimited liability for all partners.	Pass-Through All profits or losses taxed as an individual
Limited Partnership	More than one owner with no limits.	Unlimited liability for general partner. Limited liability for limited partner.	Pass-Through All profits or losses taxed as an individual
Limited Liability Partnership	More than one with no limits; however, states may limit who can register as LLP. Example: some states only allow licensed professionals to form a LLP.	Limited liability for all partners.	Pass-Through All profits or losses taxed as an individual

Sole Proprietorship

A sole proprietorship is the simplest business structure an entrepreneur may form. A sole proprietorship basically refers to a person that owns a business and is responsible for all debts. The business can operate under the person's name or it can operate under a fictitious name. A sole proprietorship is popular because of its simplicity, it is very easy to form with little cost involved in its creation. A sole proprietorship only has to register its name and secure any licenses required to operate the business, and it is ready for business. Since the sole proprietor has compete ownership of the business, a huge advantage of this form of business structure is the owner has complete control and decision-making power over the business. The biggest disadvantage is that the business owner is responsible for all liability the business incurs.

The downfall to choosing a sole proprietorship is that the business owner is personally responsible for all debts the business incurs. Creditors may sue the owner to satisfy unpaid debt, customers may sue the owner if there is poor workmanship or if the business caused the customer injury. The proprietor is also liable for any actions taken by its employees that may have caused harm to the business' customers. It is possible for the business owner to purchase liability insurance that can cover the cost of torts, injury or shoddy workmanship. However, every policy has limits on coverage and there are exclusions in the policy that may not cover unforeseen liability. It is important to consult an insurance agent to receive advice on how much liability insurance to purchase, what the policy does cover, and more importantly, what the policy does not cover.

Types of Insurance Every Business Should Consider		
General Liability Insurance	Commercial Auto Insurance	Data Breach Insurance
Property Insurance	Workers Compensation	Life Insurance
Business Interruption Insurance	Health Insurance	Disability Insurance
Professional Liability Insurance (Errors and Omission Insurance)	Product Insurance	Business Owners Policy

There are several other benefits to choosing a sole proprietorship. First and foremost is the low cost of startup as there are no legal fees or formal legal paperwork to complete. The speed at which a business can start operating is much faster when choosing a sole proprietorship over other alternatives. A sole proprietorship typically can start operations within a day to a week after formation, depending on whether a "doing business as" name needs to be registered or if the business plans to hire employees. Regardless, the startup time is much faster than any other type of business structure.

Taxation is a major concern when choosing a legal structure. A sole proprietorship takes advantage of lower individual tax rates because all profits from the business are taxed as personal income. The IRS calls this "pass-through" taxation because profits pass through the business and are taxed on the individual's personal income statement. The main difference between reporting income from a sole proprietorship than from a job is that the sole proprietor must list the profit or loss amounts on IRS Form Schedule C (Profit or Loss From a Business) and submit it along with Form 1040.

A sole proprietorship can deduct business expenses just like any other business structure including operating expenses, cost of goods sold, advertising, travel expenses, and even the costs of some meals. It is possible to write off much of the startup costs, as well as equipment and other asset expenditures. Sole proprietors can also take advantage of the pass-through deduction created by the 2017 Tax Cuts and Jobs Acts.

This pass-through deduction allows a sole proprietor to deduct up to 20% of net business income earned as an additional tax deduction. However, sole proprietors with incomes greater than $157,500 or $315,000, if married and filing jointly, must have employees or depreciable business assets to take advantage of this deduction and the deduction is limited to the percentage of employee wages or business asset costs. The deduction is not available at all to those that provide certain types of personal services and whose income exceeds $207,500 or $415,000, if married and filing jointly. Currently this deduction is available from 2018 to 2025. Check with the IRS for more information about the new Pass-Through Deduction provided by this new act from congress.

The sole proprietor may be required to make quarterly estimated income tax payments to the IRS and, in some cases, also to the state. Since the sole proprietor does not receive a regular paycheck from an employer that withholds taxes, this quarterly estimated income tax payment must be filed using IRS Form 1040-ES. Generally, the IRS requires a quarterly estimated tax payment if (1). you expect to owe more than $1000 in Federal taxes for the year, after subtracting federal tax withholdings and refundable credits, or (2). you expect federal withholdings and refundable credits to be less than the smaller of (a). 90% of the tax shown on this year's federal tax return, or (b). 100% of the tax shown on the previous year's federal tax return. Information can be found on the instruction page of IRS Form 1040-ES.

Generally if you do not pay enough tax in a timely manner either through withholding or with making estimated tax payments, you may be required to pay a penalty. For more information refer to IRS Publication 505, Tax Withholding and Estimated Tax, for a detailed discussion on underpayment penalty, in addition to exceptions to this penalty. Since a sole proprietorship is not a legal entity, there are no costs involved to start this type of structure. Therefore there are no ongoing costs to continue operating as a sole proprietorship each year. Many entrepreneurs are drawn to this type of legal structure for this reason; however, a sole proprietorship has limited flexibility when it is time to grow. As a sole proprietorship, the business owner may have difficulty securing a loan because most banks require a business to be incorporated before they will give them a loan. Additionally there is a perception issue, due to the fact that customers see an incorporated business as having a more professional appearance.

One additional drawback to a sole proprietorship is, unlike a corporation, there is no continuity of life of this type of legal structure. On the death or disability of the sole proprietor, the business terminates. If the proprietor dies, the assets will go to the proprietor's legal heirs. The heirs may continue to operate the business, but legally the business is a new startup sole proprietorship owned by the heir. A second option would be for the heirs to sell the business' assets as a going concern and the new proprietor would legally start a new business entity, even if it wanted to keep the same name. A third option would be for the heirs to sell the assets on a piecemeal basis.

Many times it is difficult to sell a sole proprietorship as going concern after the death or disability of an owner. Investors are wary that employees will not stay with the business and there is a greater concern about the loss of the proprietor's personal service, which is often a main factor in the value of the business. Due to continuity concerns, a sole proprietor should take steps early in the life of the business to address this issue. The proprietor can plan for his or her death or withdrawal from the business by entering into a buy-sell agreement with an heir, investor, relatives, or employees who will agree to take over the business when the proprietor can no longer manage day to day operations.

Bottom Line: A sole proprietorship has advantages and disadvantages. The advantages include no corporate income taxes, minimal legal costs and paperwork to form the business, and the sole proprietor has complete control over business decisions. The biggest disadvantage is the unlimited liability the proprietor faces against any debts or obligations the business owes. Also, the sole proprietor is liable for the actions of its employees as well. Other disadvantages include difficulty of obtaining financing from banks and the fact that the business dies when the proprietor dies or becomes incapacitated and can no longer operate the business.

General Partnership

A general partnership is an agreement between two or more persons to agree to share all responsibilities of owning a business which would include sharing profits and liabilities of the business. A general partnership is very similar to a sole proprietorship with the exception that in a sole proprietorship the business owner has complete control of decision-making within the business. As a general partnership, decision-making is split between all of the partners and each owner loses some control over the business; however all liability is the responsibility of both partners. The fact is that any one partner can be sued for the entirety of the business' debts.

Since a general partnership is an agreement between two or more persons, it is highly recommended that a partnership agreement be created; although a general partnership can be formed orally. In this respect, there is more paperwork required to create a general partnership than a sole proprietorship. A general partnership agreement should include the following items: contributions, distributions, transfer of ownership, decision-making procedures, dispute resolution, and dissolution.

Every general partnership agreement should clearly state each partner's stake in the company. How much did each partner invest into the formation of the business and what ongoing financial investment will be made by each partner into the business? This should include not only money, but should include time invested, customers brought into the business, and equipment, along with any other tangible or intangible asset brought into the business.

Since each partner invests into the business in order to make money, the agreement should layout how profits will be distributed. How much of the profits will be distributed to the partners? When will be profits be distributed and who will be paid first? Not only do profit payouts need to be defined, but are there going to be salaries paid to the partners and how much?

Decisions must be made as to the transfer of ownership of the business. What will happen if a partner gets disabled or dies? A buyout or transfer of ownership plan needs to be put in place so that each partner will know what is expected of them during this type of event. The agreement needs to have provisions that include retirement plans or actions taken if one partner wants to sell their interest in the partnership. Additionally, a list of circumstances should be made as to when changes in the partnership can be made and the process for making these changes.

Being in a partnership means that there will be differing viewpoints when decisions are to be made. Therefore, it is imperative to layout a decision-making process in the partnership agreement. How will day-to-day decisions and long-term decisions be made? Who will get final say in the case of a tie? What types of decisions will require a unanimous vote and which types of decisions can be made by a single partner? By coming to this understanding early in the life of the business, there will be fewer disputes later on.

No one wants to think about disputes, but disputes in a partnership can get ugly. How will disputes within the partnership be handled? When will a mediator need to step in? Lawsuits occur within partnerships, so tackling how to handle these types of situations can prevent such an extreme action.

The last item to be discussed in a partnership agreement is on what terms dissolution of the partnership should occur. This may be the option of choice if the partners cannot come to a unanimous decision on the future of the business. Many times dissolution terms are dictated by state law and this should be researched in order to define the process of dissolving the partnership.

Creating a partnership agreement takes some time and some money, but is well worth the peace of mind knowing that all partners are on the same page and have a clear understanding of how the partnership will operate. Although there are partnership templates that can be found on the internet and can be completed by the partners, it is recommended to get professional legal counsel when drawing up the agreement.

What to Include in a General Partnership Agreement	
Partnership Information Partnership name Effective date (when partnership began) Business Purpose Business Address	*Partner Information* How many partners Partners names Partners addresses
Initial Capital Contribution Initial capital partners contributed Contribution deadline (date that all contributions must be made)	*Ownership* Percentage of ownership of each partner
Profits and Losses How will partners divide profits and losses How often will profits be shared How much profit will be retained in business	*Decision Making and Management Roles* How will partners make important decisions How will ties be handled Who will handle day to day decisions
Partnership Checks Who has authority to write checks	*Vacation* How much vacation time can each partner take
Accounting Wil business use cash accounting or accrual accounting	*Governing Law* How will disputes be handled When will arbitration be used
Executing Agreement All partners and spouses (domestic partners) must sign in front of notary public	

For the most part the advantages and disadvantages of a general partnership mirror a sole proprietorship. Like a sole proprietorship, a general partnership does not pay corporate taxes. Taxes from the business are passed-through to the partners individually based on the partnership agreement, regardless of time or effort put into the business. Although the business does not pay corporate taxes, a general partnership must file an informational return, Form 1065, with the IRS each year the business is in operation. The Form 1065 must be signed by one of the partners when filing with the IRS. Along with Form 1065, the partnership must prepare forms called Schedule K and Schedule K-1. Schedule K summarizes the partner's profits and losses for the year, while Schedule K-1 shows each partner's separate share and must be filed with each partner's individual tax return.

Just like a sole proprietor, if general partners receives periodic draws from the business, they must file and pay estimated taxes quarterly. Because these draws are not subject to tax withholdings, each partner must file and pay estimated taxes with the IRS using form 1040-ES.

As stated earlier, every partner in a general partnership is responsible for all liabilities the business may incur. Regardless of time, effort or financial contribution, either partner can be sued for the entirety of a debt of financial obligation. Just like a sole proprietorship, each partner is responsible for actions of their employees and any issues from products sold or services they perform. Liability insurance can help with these costs, but there are always limits to coverage and exclusions for some types of events.

Although there are added costs involved with drawing up a partnership agreement, the agreement can help with continuance of operations if one of the partners can no longer perform their duties for the business. The partnership agreement can also help with the business' ability to handle future needs. A well-written agreement discusses, the decision-making process for long-term goals, such as expansion and growth. In these ways, a general partnership has an advantage over a sole proprietorship.

Bottom Line: There are advantages and disadvantages to a general partnership. The advantages include (1). not having to pay corporate income taxes, income is passed-through to the partners, (2). easy to establish, costs mostly involve creating a partnership agreement, and (3). having partners increases the pool of skills, knowledge and customers brought to the business. Disadvantages to a general partnership include (1). partners are jointly and severely liable for debts and actions of the business, either partner can be sued for the entire obligation, (2). a partner cannot transfer ownership without the consent of all other partners, and (3). partnerships can become unstable because there is a possibility of dissolution if one partner dies or decides to leave the business.

Limited Partnership

A limited partnership (LP) is a partnership arrangement where one or more partners provide financial backing for the business (limited partner) and one or more other partners are involved in the day-to-day decision-making and operations of the business (general partner). The difference between a general partnership and a limited partnership is the liability of the limited partner. The limited partner, sometimes known as a silent partner, is only liable for the amount of money invested in the business. The general partner, who makes the day-to-day decisions for the business is responsible for all other liability the business incurs.

The advantage for liability for the limited partner turns into a disadvantages because the limited partner gives away rights for day-to-day decision-making for the business. The costs of forming a limited partnership can be higher than a general partnership because an attorney should be hired to customize a partnership's operating agreement, which is a contract that dictates how the business is to be operated. The agreement should include all of the criteria that is in a general partnership agreement and should include provisions for contributions of funds, distribution of profits, transfer of ownership, decision-making procedures, dispute resolution, and dissolution.

A Certificate of Limited Partnership must be filed with the state prior to the business coming into existence. This may also include paying state filing fees which varies by state. It is important to check each state's requirements for filing this certificate.

Tax advantages for a limited partnership are the same as a general partnership. There are no corporate income taxes, profits and losses are passed-through to the partners and are to be filed with each partner's individual tax return. Just like the general partnership, a limited partnership must file Form 1065 and must complete and file Schedule K with the IRS and submit Schedule K-1 with the owner's personal income tax forms.

If a limited investor decides to become more involved in the day-to-day operations of the business, they become a general partner and will take on general partner liability. A limited partner needs to take this into consideration before making this move.

Bottom Line: Other than the liability of the limited partner, the limited partnership's advantages and disadvantages are similar to a general partnership. The advantages include no corporate income taxes for the business, profits and losses are passed-through to each partner's individual income statement. It is easier to attract investors to a limited partnership due to limited risk from liability. Limited partners also get to share in profits and losses without having to participate in business operations. The biggest advantage for the general partner is the control of day-to-day operations, while the biggest disadvantage for the general partner is unlimited liability for all debt and obligations incurred by the business.

Limited Liability Partnership

A limited liability partnership (LLP) is similar to a limited partnership, but there are no general partners. All partners have limited liability based on their investment in the business. A limited liability partnership is well suited for profession organizations such a law firms. In some states a LLP can only be formed by professionals. Limited liability partnerships are formed because partners do not want the risk of liability from other partners, such as professional malpractice. In some states such as California, professionals are required to form an LLP, because they are prohibited from forming a corporation such as a limited liability company (LLC).

The partnership must file a Certificate of Limited Liability Partnership with the state and pay the accompanying fees. Just as for a limited partnership, each state has its own rules for forming a LLP and it is recommended to check with the state for the appropriate laws.

Bottom Line: A limited liability partnership is the same as a limited partnership other than the reduction of risk liability for all partners.

General Partnership vs. Limited Partnership vs. Limited Liability Partnership
Why choose a general partnership (GP)?
Ease of creation
Low cost of operation
Few ongoing requirements
Why choose a limited partnership (LP)?
Unlimited liability for general partners only
Limited partner's liability limited to amount invested in partnership
Limited partner not involved with management of business
LP's are structure of choice for short-term projects/ventures
Why choose limited liability partnership (LLP)?
Professional service business – most states limit formation of LLPs to professional groups
Personal asset protection – each partner only responsible for own malpractice, not any of other partner's liability

Chapter 3

Incorporated Legal Business Structures

Incorporating a business is one of the best ways to protect your personal wealth. By incorporating a business, the business owner gains protection from many of the risks that comes from liability within a business. As a corporation, a business has five main advantages including protection of personal assets, easier access to capital, additional credibility for the company, perpetual existence, and anonymity for owners of the business. Forming a corporation is the most complex of legal business structures. Incorporated legal business structures include limited liability company (LLC), S corporation and C corporation. In this chapter we will discuss the differences along with the advantages and disadvantages of each. See Appendix A for a quick reference guide for choosing a legal business structure.

Type of Structure	Number of Owners	Liability	Taxation
Limited Liability Company (LLC)	There can be as few as one member (single member LLC) or an unlimited number of members (multi-member LLC).	Limited liability for all members.	Pass-Through to members. All profits or losses taxed as an individual
Subchapter S Corporation	There can be as few as one shareholder, but is limited to 100 total shareholders.	Limited liability for all shareholders.	Pass-Through to shareholders. All profits or losses taxed as an individual
C Corporation	There can be as few as one shareholder and there is no limit to the number of shareholders.	Limited liability for all shareholders.	Profits taxed at corporate tax rate. After tax profits distributed to shareholders in form of dividends and are taxed individually at qualified dividend tax rate.

Limited Liability Company (LLC)

A limited liability company (LLC) is a legal business structure that has the advantage of limited legal liability of a corporation, along with the unincorporated feature of pass-through taxation. Like a partnership or sole proprietorship, the business is not taxed at a corporate tax rate, instead profits and losses are passed-through to the owner's individual tax return and taxed at the individual tax rate. Owners of a LLC are called members.

For single member (owner) LLC's, the IRS treats the company as a sole proprietorship for tax purposes. The LLC does not pay corporate taxes nor do they have to file a return with the IRS. As the single proprietor of a LLC, the owner will report all profits or losses on IRS Schedule C and submit the form along with Form 1040, their individual tax return.

Multi-member LLC's are treated as partnerships for tax purposes by the IRS. The company does not pay an income tax, but each member is required to pay taxes on their share of profits on their personal income statement using Schedule E for profit or loss declaration. The business is required to file Form 1065 with the IRS, which is the same as a partnership.   Along with Form 1065, the LLC must prepare forms called Schedule K and Schedule K-1. Schedule K summarizes the member's profits and losses for the year, while Schedule K-1 shows each member's separate share and must be filed with each member's individual tax return.

The Following Can Be Members (Owners) Of A Limited Liability Company (LLC)	
U. S. Citizens	Non U. S. Citizens
U. S. Residents	Non U. S. Residents
U. S. Immigrants	U. S. Foreigners
Other LLCs	S Corporations
C Corporations	Other Legal Entities (besides corporations)
Trusts	Pension Plans
Individual Retirement Accounts (IRAs)	

If the LLC needs to regularly keep a substantial amount of profits in the business the company may be able to benefit by electing corporate taxation. Any LLC can choose to file as a corporation by filing IRS Form 8839, *Entity Classification Election*, and checking the corporate tax treatment box. If an LLC chooses to file as a corporation, then it can have an unlimited amount of members. With the passage of the Tax Cuts and Jobs Act of 2017, corporate tax rates are 21%, which is lower than the top three individual tax rates that range from 32% to 37%. However, when the profit, after the corporate taxes has been paid, is distributed to the member(s), it is subject to double taxation. This money is taxed a second time at the individual tax rate, so the corporate tax savings could be wiped away.

Additionally, LLC members are considered self-employed and are not subject to tax withholdings. Therefore, just as a sole proprietorship or partnership, the member is required file and pay quarterly estimated taxes using IRS Form 1040-ES.

The main advantage of a LLC is the limits placed on liability for its members. Typically, exposure to liability for the member of a LLC is limited to the member's investment. Of course there are always exceptions, and many times additional insurance can be purchased for added protection. An added feature is that in some states, the business interest of members of the LLC are protected from claims from the member's personal creditors. This advantage is not applicable to corporations or limited liability partnerships. Members should check with local state laws for more information about these protections.

Creation of a limited liability company is formed under state law. The cost for formation and maintenance of a LLC is typically lower than that of a corporation. To create a LLC requires the owners to file Articles of Organization with the state. The Articles of Organization acts like a charter and sets out basic information about the company such as company name, statement of purpose, duration of operation, principle place of business, whether member managed or non-member managed, and name and address of a registered agent. The registered agent must be located in the state the LLC is formed and that person will receive important tax and legal information on behalf of the LLC.

Articles of Organization templates are available from each state's corporation commission website or Secretary of State's website. You can find your state's template from the list of websites listed by state in Appendix B of this book. Although each state's template is different, most of the information required is the same. A sample Articles of Organization template from the state of Virginia is found in Appendix C in this book. Most LLC's Articles of Organization are two pages, although some, like Virginia, are only one page long. The templates include instructions on how to fill them out, where to send them to, along with all required fees.

In addition to filing the Articles of Organization the LLC must pay a filing fee to the state, usually between $100 and $800. The members then create an operating agreement which declares the rights and responsibilities of each member. Some states require the LLC to publish a notice of intent to form a LLC. It is important to check with your states regulations for forming a LLC.

Bottom Line: A limited liability company is considered a hybrid of a partnership and a corporation. The LLC offers the limited liability features of a corporation, while taking the advantage of pass-through taxation like a partnership. Other advantages include (1). members are allowed to participate fully in the management of the company, (2). corporations and partners can be a member of a LLC, (3). there is no limit to the number of members in a LLC, but a LLC can have only one member, (4). a LLC offers a great amount of flexibility, because members can decide how to operate various aspects of the business through the operating agreement, and (5). a LLC may be classified as a sole proprietorship, a partnership, or a corporation for tax purposes. The downside of an LLC is the complexity required to form the business entity.

Subchapter S Corporation

A subchapter S corporation (S corporation) is a legal business structure in the form of a corporation that meets specific IRS requirements and has the benefit of pass-through taxation similar to a partnership. Similar to a sole proprietorship, partnership, and a LLC, the S corporation is not taxed as a corporation, instead profits and losses are passed-through to the individual owner and is taxed at an individual tax rate.

There are certain requirements that must be met before an S corporation can be formed. First an S corporation may have no more than 75 shareholders. When calculating the 75 shareholder limit, a husband and wife counts as one shareholder. Additionally, only the following entity classifications can be a shareholder: individuals, estates, certain trusts, certain partnerships, tax-exempt charitable organizations, and other S corporations (only if the other S corporation is the sole shareholder).

An additional benefit of an S corporation is if the company does not have inventory, they can choose the cash method of accounting, which is much simpler than the accrual method. Under the cash method, income is taxable when received and expenses are deductible when paid. C corporations do not have this advantage.

S corporations face the same requirements for formation that C corporations require. An S corporation must first file Articles of Incorporation with the state it incorporates in. The Articles of Incorporation, sometimes known as Articles of Association, Certificate of Incorporation or Corporate Charter, is a document that establishes the existence of a corporation. The document typically includes the following information: name of the corporation, name and address of the registered agent, type of corporate organization (for profit, non-profit, non-stock, professional, etc.), names and addresses of board members, duration of corporation, and a statement of the firm's purpose. In addition to the Articles of Incorporation, the company must submit the state's required forms along with all associated fees. Each year the S corporation must renew its existence with the state and pay all associated fees.

Like Articles of Organization, Articles of Incorporation templates are available from each state's corporation commission website or Secretary of State's website. You can find your state's template from the list of websites listed by state in Appendix B of this book. Although each state's template is different, most of the information required is the same. A sample Articles of Incorporation template from the state of Virginia is found in Appendix D in this book. Most Articles of Incorporation are two pages, although some, like Virginia, are only one page long. The templates include instructions on how to fill them out, where to send them to, along with all required fees.

Like a C corporation, an S corporation shareholders must elect a board of directors, hold director and shareholder meetings, keep corporate minutes, and allow shareholders to vote on major corporate decisions. The legal costs of formation and accounting costs are the same as C corporations and are typically more expensive than a LLC. Unlike a C corporation, an S corporation can only issue common stock, which can hamper the firm's ability to raise capital.

An S corporation protects personal assets from debts and claims made against the business. In theory an S corporation has limited liability, only the shareholder's monetary investment is at risk. However, there can be some exceptions. If the company acquired debt or had claims as an unincorporated business prior to becoming an S corporation, then those obligations have no protection from personal assets. If an S corporation acquires a bank loan using personal assets as collateral, then those assets may be forfeited. Many times banks and vendors require a shareholder to sign a personal guarantee, then the shareholder's personal assets are at risk. Personal protection from liability is at risk if the court finds that the corporation, in practice, is not acting separately from the owners. Finally, limited liability of an S corporation does not protect a shareholder from personal liability arising from that shareholders own misconduct, such as committing fraud.

Taxation for an S corporation is similar to a LLC, because profits and losses are passed-through the business to the shareholder(s). Therefore, an S corporation pays no corporate income tax. The S corporation must file Form 1120-S with the IRS by March 15th, this form cannot be filed with your personal income taxes. The S corporation must distribute Schedule K-1 to its shareholders and the shareholders submit Schedule K-1 with their personal tax return IRS Form 1040 by April 15th.

An S corporation has the advantage of having continuity of life. Unlike a sole proprietorship, an S corporation lives on after the death or disablement of the founder. An S corporation can die, if the company fails to renew their annual required filings, which includes annual fees.

A corporation can choose to move between an S corporation and a C corporation as long as it follows the IRS guidelines. A C corporation can change to an S corporation as long as it chooses that election no later than two months and 15 days after the first day of the taxable year. An S corporation may revoke its status by either failing to meet the requirements of eligibility for subchapter S corporations or by filing with the IRS no later than two months and 15 days after the first day of the taxable year. Once changing to a C corporation, the business' profits will be taxed as a corporation.

Bottom Line: A business electing a legal structure of a subchapter S corporation enjoys the limited liability of a C corporation, while taking advantage of pass-through taxation that a LLC enjoys. An S corporation avoids double taxation by not having to pay corporate income tax. The disadvantage of an S corporation is the cost and paperwork required to form. An S corporation must file Articles of Incorporation with the state along with the associated fees. Additionally, the corporation must renew their status each year and pay the associated fees. It is also important to keep in mind that decisions are based on the size of a shareholder's stake in the company. The larger shareholders have more voting power and have a bigger voice in business decisions.

C Corporations

A C corporation is a legal business structure that limits the liability of its shareholders, but with a disadvantage of double taxation. The business pays corporate taxes and the income is taxed again when it is distributed to the individual shareholders. The upside to the C corporation is the ability to reinvest profits back into the business at a lower corporate income tax rate. Most large businesses choose to become C corporations.

A C corporation has no restrictions on ownership and have an unlimited growth potential, thanks to the ability to sell stock. Unlike an S corporation, a C corporation has no limits as to who or what can own a stock in the corporation. The costs and paperwork required to form and maintain a C corporation is the same as an S corporation. Just as an S corporation, a C corporation must file Articles of Incorporation, submit the appropriate state required paperwork and pay all associated fees. Each year the C corporation must renew its application and pay all associated fees.

Like an S corporation, a C corporation uses the same Articles of Incorporation templates that are available from each state's corporation commission website or Secretary of State's website. You can find your state's template from the list of websites listed by state in Appendix B of this book. Although each state's template is different, most of the information required is the same. A sample Articles of Incorporation template from the state of Virginia is found in Appendix D in this book. Most Articles of Incorporation are two pages, although some, like Virginia, are only one page long. The templates include instructions on how to fill them out, where to send them to, along with all required fees.

A big advantage of corporations, both S and C, is limited liability. However with a C corporation the limited liability expands to directors, officers, shareholders, and employees. Although there is limited liability to shareholders based on the amount of the investment, there are still areas that can affect a person's personal liability. These specific areas of liability include: a shareholder who injures someone personally, a shareholder who has signed a personal guarantee with a bank or vendor, a person (shareholder, director, etc.) fails to pay payroll withholdings to the IRS, there is a commission of intentional fraud, a person treats the business as an extension of themselves rather than a separate business entity, or the court rules the corporation ceases to exist.

A C corporation is the only legal business structure that has double taxation. The business must first pay income taxes on profits at the company level and then the same money is taxed again when it is dispersed to the shareholders in the form of dividends. The C corporation must file IRS Form 1020 and pay any associated taxes based on company profits. The corporation must send its stockholders IRS Form 1099-DIV to reflect the amount of dividends paid. The stockholder must file this form with their personal income taxes. One disadvantage to a C corporation is that shareholders cannot take advantage of business losses as an S corporation can. An S corporation can deduct all business losses from their personal income reporting.

It is much easier for a C corporations to raise funds because there is no limits to ownership and no limits to the number of stockholders. It is also easier for an incorporated business to get loans from banks. Additionally, C corporations have enhanced credibility from both lenders and suppliers. A C corporation can also go public and issue an initial public offering (IPO) in order to raise funds. In order to issue an IPO the business must follow certain steps regarding SEC regulations and ownership should consult with an investment banker to proceed with such plans.

A C corporation has a perpetual existence; therefore, the business does not die when the owner dies or can no longer take part in day-to-day operations. It is easy to transfer ownership of a C corporation by selling the stock held with the business.

Bottom Line: Two primary reasons to use a C corporation legal business structure is the limited liability feature and the unlimited growth potential through the sale of stocks. Other benefits of a C corporation include perpetual existence, enhanced credibility, and an easier ability to raise funds through bank loans. The biggest disadvantage of a C corporation is the double taxation of profits, but other disadvantages include the cost and paperwork required to form, no personal deduction for corporate losses, and more government oversight especially if the business is publicly traded.

Limited Liability Company (LLC) vs. Corporation		
Criteria	LLC	Corporation
Shields Personal Assets from business liability	Yes	Yes
Requires separation of personal finances from business finances	Yes	Yes
Allowable in all 50 states and the District of Columbia	Yes	Yes
Highly flexible management structure	Yes	No
Flexible tax reporting options	Yes	No
Preferred by outside investors	No	Yes
Preferred for IPO	No	Yes
Recognized outside the United States	No	Yes

S Corporation vs. C Corporation		
Criteria	S Corp	C Corp
Owners pay personal income tax on distributions from business	Yes	Yes
Business must pay corporate income tax	No	Yes
All business income/loss is passed-through to owners each year	Yes	No
No more than 100 shareholders	Yes	No
Shareholder must be U. S. citizen or U. S. resident	Yes	No

You do not have to decide between an S corporation or C corporation right away. You have 75 days after forming business to file with the IRS.

Chapter 4

Steps To Form Legal Business Structures

There are different steps involved to form each type of business structure. In this chapter, the basic steps to form each type of legal business structure will be discussed. Keep in mind there are specific differences between states that should be considered before beginning the process of forming your business.

Sole Proprietorship

To form a sole proprietorship there are no formal or legal steps to take at the federal, state, or local level. However depending on the city or municipality your business is in, the business may have to be registered or there may be certain licenses that must be obtained. The following is a list of items that should be considered when starting a sole proprietorship.

1. Select a business name.
   a. Register your name. If you plan to operate your business under your own name you can skip this step; however, if you plan to operate under a fictitious name, doing business as (DBA), it should be registered. Check with the local government (clerk of court) to register your name.
   b. When creating you name, think about a domain name if you plan to create a website.
   c. Trademark your name. This is not mandatory, but it is a good idea to give you legal protection so that no one else can use your name.
2. Separate your personal finances from your business finances.
   a. Open a business bank account.
   b. Get a business credit card/debit card.
   c. Start separate business accounting records.
3. Obtain any required business licenses and permits.

4. Prepare to report taxes.
   a. If you have employees, obtain an employer identification number (EIN). Pay quarterly payroll taxes.
   b. Prepare to pay quarterly estimated tax payments using IRS Form 1040-ES.
   c. When filing year end federal taxes use Schedule C, which is part of IRS Form 1040 to report yearly income.
5. Purchase insurance.
   a. Worker's Compensation Insurance if you have employees.
   b. Business liability insurance to protect your property and assets.
   c. Disability insurance to protect income if you cannot work.

General Partnership

A general partnership is one of the easiest legal business structures to create and formed by two or more partners. The following are the steps required to form a general partnership.

1. Select a business name.
   a. Register your name. If you plan to operate your business under your partnership name you can skip this step; however, if you plan to operate under a fictitious name, doing business as (DBA), it should be registered. Check with the local government (clerk of court) to register your name.
   b. When creating you name, think about a domain name if you plan to create a website.
   c. Trademark your name. This is not mandatory, but it is a good idea to give you legal protection so that no one else can use your name.
2. Create a partnership agreement.
   a. Detail the rights and responsibilities of each partner.
   b. Agreement on how a partner can leave, be removed, along with what will happen upon death of a partner.
   c. How revenues will be shared.
   d. Procedures for dispute resolution.
3. File partnership with the state.
   a. Most states do not require a partnership agreement.
   b. However, it is recommended that the partnership file with the state in order to provide public notice of basic information about the partnership, such as agency authorization of the partners.
4. Obtain an employer identification number (EIN) - This is required to open a bank account or hire employees.
5. Obtain any required business licenses and permits.

6. Prepare to report taxes.
   a. If you have employees, pay quarterly payroll taxes.
   b. Prepare to pay quarterly estimated tax payments using IRS Form 1040-ES.
   c. When filing year end federal taxes use Schedule K-1, which is attached to IRS Form 1040 to report yearly income.
7. Purchase insurance.
   a. Worker's Compensation Insurance if you have employees.
   b. Business liability insurance to protect your property and assets.
   c. Disability insurance to protect income if you cannot work.

Limited Partnership

A limited partnership requires at least one limited partner and at least one general partner. The following is the procedure to create a limited partnership.

1. Select a business name.
    a. Register your name. If you plan to operate your business under your partnership name you can skip this step; however, if you plan to operate under a fictitious name, doing business as (DBA), it should be registered. Check with the local government (clerk of court) to register your name.
    b. When creating you name, think about a domain name if you plan to create a website.
    c. Trademark your name. This is not mandatory, but it is a good idea to give you legal protection so that no one else can use your name.
2. Create a limited partnership agreement. - A limited partnership agreement is not required by most states, but it is highly recommended.
    a. Detail the rights and responsibilities of each partner.
    b. Agreement on how a partner can leave, be removed, along with what will happen upon death of a partner.
    c. How revenues will be shared.
    d. Procedures for dispute resolution.
3. Designate a registered agent.
    a. Some states require a limited partnership to have and maintain a registered agent. A registered agent is a resident of that state who is legally authorized to do business within that state.

4. File a certificate of limited partnership with state.
   a. This certificate is mandatory in every state.
   b. Depending on the state in which it is filed, the certificate of limited partnership requires basic information about the business which includes entity address, agents name and address, names and addresses of partners.
   c. Typically forms can be found on Secretary of State's website.
   d. Filing fees range from $50 to $100
5. Obtain an employer identification number (EIN).
6. Obtain a state identification number. – Although not required by all states, this helps classify the business for the state.
7. Obtain any required business licenses and permits.
8. Prepare to report taxes.
   a. If you have employees, pay quarterly payroll taxes.
   b. Prepare to pay quarterly estimated tax payments using IRS Form 1040-ES.
   c. When filing year end federal taxes use Schedule K-1, which is attached to IRS Form 1040 to report yearly income.
9. Purchase insurance.
   a. Worker's Compensation Insurance if you have employees.
   b. Business liability insurance to protect your property and assets.
   c. Disability insurance to protect income if you cannot work.

Limited Liability Partnership

A limited liability partnership allows partners to enjoy limited liability protection and the tax benefits of a limited partnership. Some states will only allow professional groups, such as lawyers, to form a LLP. The following is the procedure to form a limited liability partnership.

1. Verify ability to qualify for a LLP. Check with specific states before applying.
2. Select a business name.
   a. Register your name. If you plan to operate your business under your partnership name you can skip this step; however, if you plan to operate under a fictitious name, doing business as (DBA), it should be registered. Check with the local government (clerk of court) to register your name.
   b. When creating you name, think about a domain name if you plan to create a website.
   c. Trademark your name. This is not mandatory, but it is a good idea to give you legal protection so that no one else can use your name.
3. Create a limited liability partnership agreement. - A limited liability partnership agreement is not required by most states, but it is highly recommended.
   a. Detail the rights and responsibilities of each partner.
   b. Agreement on how a partner can leave, be removed, along with what will happen upon death of a partner.
   c. How revenues will be shared.
   d. Procedures for dispute resolution.
4. Designate a registered agent.
   a. Some states require a limited liability partnership to have and maintain a registered agent. A registered agent is a resident of that state who is legally authorized to do business within that state.

5. File a certificate of limited liability partnership with state.
   a. This certificate is mandatory in every state.
   b. Depending on the state in which it is filed, the certificate of limited liability partnership requires basic information about the business which includes entity address, agents name and address, names and addresses of partners.
   c. Typically forms can be found on Secretary of State's website.
   d. Filing fees range from $50 to $100
6. Obtain an employer identification number (EIN).
7. Obtain a state identification number. – Although not required by all states, this helps classify the business for the state.
8. Obtain required licenses and permits.
9. Fulfill Publication Requirements. – Some states require LLPs to publicize formation. See state's individual requirements.
10. Prepare to report taxes.
    a. If you have employees, pay quarterly payroll taxes.
    b. Prepare to pay quarterly estimated tax payments using IRS Form 1040-ES.
    c. When filing year end federal taxes use Schedule K-1, which is attached to IRS Form 1040 to report yearly income.
11. Purchase insurance.
    a. Worker's Compensation Insurance if you have employees.
    b. Business liability insurance to protect your property and assets. Malpractice insurance is needed for many professional groups.
    d. Disability insurance to protect income if you cannot work.

Limited Liability Company

A limited liability company can provide a variety of benefits to its members (owners). These benefits include limited liability to its members, along with tax advantages. Organizing a LLC requires careful steps to comply with state government regulations. Check with your individual state to meet all requirements. Below is the basic steps to follow when creating a LLC.

1. Select a business name.
   a. Register your name. If you plan to operate your business under your LLC's name you can skip this step; however, if you plan to operate under a fictitious name, doing business as (DBA), it should be registered. Check with the local government (clerk of court) to register your name.
   b. When creating you name, think about a domain name if you plan to create a website.
   c. Trademark your name. This is not mandatory, but it is a good idea to give you legal protection so that no one else can use your name.
2. File articles of organization.
   a. Prepare and file articles of organization from your state's LLC commissioning office. See Appendix B
   b. Typically, the articles of organization consists of the LLC's name, address, and the names of owners, called members.
   c. Some states call this requirement articles of formation or certificate of organization.
3. Create an LLC operating agreement.
   a. Similar to a partnership agreement, the LLC operating agreement consists of the rules of operation that govern the company.
   b. A typical LLC operating agreement includes percentage of ownership of members, member's rights and responsibilities, and requirements for decision making, management and how to disperse profits and losses.

4. Publish a notice where required.
   a. Although not required by most states, some states require a notice to be published in a local newspaper stating the intent to start a LLC.
5. Designate a registered agent.
   a. Some states require a LLC to have and maintain a registered agent. A registered agent is a resident of that state who is legally authorized to do business within that state.
6. Obtain any required business licenses and permits.
7. Obtain an employer identification number (EIN).
8. Prepare to report taxes.
   a. If you have employees, pay quarterly payroll taxes.
   b. Prepare to pay quarterly estimated tax payments using IRS Form 1040-ES.
   c. When filing year end federal taxes use Schedule K-1, which is attached to IRS Form 1040 to report yearly income.
9. Purchase insurance.
   a. Worker's Compensation Insurance if you have employees.
   b. Business liability insurance to protect your property and assets.
   c. Disability insurance to protect income if you cannot work.
10. Retain your LLC status.
    a. In order to retain a LLC members must follow certain formalities including keeping detailed financial records, and recording minutes of major decisions.
    b. File annual reports to keep LLC in good standing with the state.

Subchapter S Corporations

Similar to a limited liability company, an S corporation can provide a variety of benefits to its shareholders (owners). These benefits include limited liability to shareholders, in addition to tax advantages. Organizing an S corporation requires careful steps to comply with state government regulations. Check with your individual state to meet all requirements. Below is the basic steps to follow when creating an S corporation.

1. Select a business name.
   a. When choosing a corporate name it cannot be the same as another corporation on file with the state corporation office. The name must end with a corporate designator of the following words "corporation", "incorporated", "limited", or the following abbreviations "corp.", "inc.", "ltd." The name cannot have wording that suggest the federal government or a restricted type of business, such as bank, national, federal, united states, or reserve.
   b. Register your name. If you plan to operate your business under your corporate name you can skip this step; however, if you plan to operate under a fictitious name, doing business as (DBA), it should be registered. Check with the local government (clerk of court) to register your name.
   c. When creating you name, think about a domain name if you plan to create a website.
   d. Trademark your name. This is not mandatory, but it is a good idea to give you legal protection so that no one else can use your name.
2. Appoint the initial directors of the corporation.
3. File the articles of incorporation with the state corporate commission office or secretary of state. See Appendix B.
   a. Include a filing fee of $100 to $800 based on requirements of state.

4. Create corporate bylaws.
   a. Corporate bylaws define a company's purpose, how it will operate and define duties of responsibility for the stockholders and those that run the corporation.
5. Designate a registered agent.
   a. Some states require an S corporation to have and maintain a registered agent. A registered agent is a resident of that state who is legally authorized to do business within that state.
6. After incorporating, file IRS Form 2553 to elect S corporation status.
7. Hold the first meeting of the board of directors.
8. Issue stock certificates to the shareholders of the corporation.
9. Obtain any required business licenses and permits.
10. Obtain an employer identification number (EIN).
11. Prepare to report taxes.
    a. If you have employees, pay quarterly payroll taxes.
    b. Shareholders prepare to pay quarterly estimated tax payments using IRS Form 1040-ES.
    c. S corporation must file IRS Form 1020-S to submit year-end tax report to IRS, along with Schedule K. When shareholders file their year-end federal taxes, they use Schedule K-1, which is attached to IRS Form 1040 to report yearly personal income.
12. Purchase insurance.
    a. Worker's Compensation Insurance if you have employees.
    b. Business liability insurance to protect your property and assets.
    c. Disability insurance to protect income if you cannot work.
13. Retain your corporation status.
    a. In order to retain a corporation status, the business must follow certain formalities including keeping detailed financial records, and recording minutes of major decisions.
    b. File annual reports to keep corporation in good standing with the state.

C Corporation

A C corporation is the most common type of legal business structure for large businesses. The major benefit to the C corporation is the ability to reinvest profits back into the business at a lower corporate income tax rate. Organizing a C corporation requires careful steps to comply with state government regulations. Check with your individual state to meet all requirements. Below is the basic steps to follow when creating a C corporation.

1. Select a business name.
   a. When choosing a corporate name it cannot be the same as another corporation on file with the state corporation office. The name must end with a corporate designator of the following words "corporation", "incorporated", "limited", or the following abbreviations "corp.", "inc.", "ltd." The name cannot have wording that suggest the federal government or a restricted type of business, such as bank, national, federal, united states, or reserve.
   b. Register your name. If you plan to operate your business under your corporate name you can skip this step; however, if you plan to operate under a fictitious name, doing business as (DBA), it should be registered. Check with the local government (clerk of court) to register your name.
   c. When creating you name, think about a domain name if you plan to create a website.
   d. Trademark your name. This is not mandatory, but it is a good idea to give you legal protection so that no one else can use your name.
2. Appoint the initial directors of the corporation.
3. File the articles of incorporation with the state corporate commission office. See Appendix B.
   a. Include a filing fee of $100 to $800 based on requirements of state.

4. Create corporate bylaws.
   a. Corporate bylaws define a company's purpose, how it will operate and define duties of responsibility for the stockholders and those that run the corporation.
5. Designate a registered agent.
   a. Some states require a C corporation to have and maintain a registered agent. A registered agent is a resident of that state who is legally authorized to do business within that state.
6. Hold the first meeting of the board of directors.
7. Issue stock certificates to the shareholders of the corporation.
8. Obtain any required business licenses and permits.
9. Obtain an employer identification number (EIN).
10. Prepare to report taxes.
    a. If you have employees, pay quarterly payroll taxes.
    b. The corporation must prepare to pay quarterly estimated tax payments using IRS Form.
    c. C corporations must file IRS Form 1020 to submit year-end tax report to IRS. When shareholders file their year-end federal taxes, they use Form 1099-DIV, which is attached to IRS Form 1040 to report yearly personal income.
11. Purchase insurance.
    a. Worker's Compensation Insurance if you have employees.
    b. Business liability insurance to protect your property and assets.
12. Retain your corporation status.
    a. In order to retain a corporation status, the business must follow certain formalities including keeping detailed financial records, and recording minutes of major decisions.
    b. File annual reports to keep corporation in good standing with the state.

Chapter 5

Incorporation Will Not Protect Against All Liability

Choosing to incorporate your business or choosing protections from limited partnerships do not save you from all liability. There are certain events that can allow creditors or individuals to make claims against your personal assets. This chapter will discuss many of these types of events.

Piercing the Corporate Veil

"Piercing the corporate veil" refers to a situation where a court order sets aside the limited liability protections provided to a corporation and hold shareholders and/or directors personally liable for the company's actions or debts. The laws differ by states, but typically is only used when there is serious misconduct by the corporation.

One of the major factors courts look at when determining if the "veil should be pierced" is existence of fraud, wrong doing, or injustice to a third party. An example of fraud would be if ABC corp. gets a large judgment it cannot pay, decides to close operations, but before closing operations, it transfers all assets to XYZ corp. This fraudulent action could lead to shareholder's personal liability for judgements against this corporation. The takeaway is that if any business action seems questionable, it is best to seek legal advice prior to taking that action.

The veil could also be pierced if there is a failure to maintain a separate identity of multiple companies. If several related affiliate businesses act under the umbrella of one company and there is a failure to maintain separate identities of the affiliated companies. An example would be if a parent company operates and controls a subsidiary by providing all financing, has the same officers, and files consolidated taxes with the subsidiary. To avoid this scenario, a parent company must make sure the subsidiary companies have separate bank accounts, separate contracts, etc.

Similarly, "piercing the veil" would include companies that fail to maintain a separate identity from its owners or shareholders. Instead of being intertwined with subsidiaries, this would entail a company that is not separated from its owners or shareholders. This situation can arise when a corporation is formed and the owner still operates out of individual checking accounts, fails to follow corporate formalities, and uses company assets as individual assets.

"Piercing the veil" could also arise if a business was not adequately capitalized. Typically a business is not punished for not making enough money, but if the courts find that the owners/shareholders did not provide enough assets to be fair to its creditors, then personal liability could be jeopardized.

A final way to "pierce the veil" is to not follow corporate formalities. Based on the type of legal structure formed (LLC, C corporation, etc.), the owners should be aware of what formalities are required by their state. Some typical corporate formalities include properly updating bylaws, maintaining stock or membership ledgers, and holding initial and annual meetings. It is important for owners to understand and follow all formalities based on the state they are incorporated in.

Personal Guarantees

 Owners of young or small businesses are often required to sign personal guarantees when signing a bank loan, rental agreements, or vendor agreements until the business can build its own credit. A personal guarantee requires the business owner to personally pay back any debt or obligation using personal assets if the business does not pay the liability. By signing the document, the owner is giving up all liability coverage the corporation provides.

Whenever possible, a business owner should avoid signing a personal guarantee. However, it sometimes becomes necessary to do so in order to keep the business moving forward. Some states have community property laws that protect property that is owned jointly with another individual. This can protect a person that signs a personal guarantee because it will shield these assets from creditors. An example would be if one spouse signs a personal guarantee and owns a house jointly with the other spouse. In a community property state, the house cannot be taken by the creditor if the obligations from the personal guarantee are not met. If your state has common property laws, both spouses should never sign a personal guarantee.

Signing a Contract in Your Own Name

Sometimes signing a personal guarantee is unavoidable, but many times giving up limited liability is caused by simple carelessness. It is extremely important to understand if you are signing a contract as an individual or a representative of the business. It can make a huge difference in the eyes of the court. If you sign the contract as "James Smith" instead of "James Smith, CEO of Smith's Plumbing Inc.", then you are signing as an individual instead of a representative of the corporation. This means you will be personally responsible for all obligations of this contract. Make sure to sign all contacts as an owner or officer of the corporation.

Use Your Own Credit Card to Fund a Purchase

Many times a small business will intertwine business and personal finances. If you use your personal credit card or home equity loan to finance any part of the business, you will be personally responsible to pay all debts owed. This can also be true even if the business name is on the credit card. You should check the original terms of the credit card application to make sure you are not personally responsible for the debt.

You Commit a Crime or Misrepresent Yourself

Corporate liability protection will not help if you break the law. It also will not protect you if you lie about anything on a loan or credit application for the business. You will probably be held personally liable for all obligations.

Your Actions Injure Some Person

If you provide a service to someone, for example a doctor, driver, consultant, accountant, etc., you can be held personally responsible for malpractice or negligence. For this reason it is recommended to take out adequate liability insurance coverage to protect against these types of claims.

Bottom Line. Incorporating, forming a LLC or limited liability partnership will not protect you from all events, but it is a good first step toward minimizing personal liability. Many times common sense approaches to events, such as seeking legal counsel will also provide protections. Business owners should also seek advice from qualified insurance professionals and go through periodic insurance reviews to make sure they are maintaining adequate coverage.

Chapter 6

Tax Treatment and the Tax Cuts and Jobs Act of 2017

When choosing a legal business structure it is important to take into consideration the treatment of taxes for your business income and your personal income. If choosing an unincorporated business, all business income (profits and losses) will be passed-through to your personal income and you will be taxed at your personal income tax rate. An S corporation has the same tax treatment as an unincorporated business. A C corporation is treated differently. A C corporation's business income will be taxed at a corporate income tax rate and dividends (profits dispersed to shareholders) are taxed at an individual tax rate. A Limited Liability Company (LLC) is taxed the same as an unincorporated business where business income and losses are passed-through to members and reported as individual income. However, a LLC can elect to be taxed the same as a C corporation. The choice of business structure can have a great impact on the amount of money business owners keep in their pocket.

Most small businesses lose money the first few years of operation. As a matter of fact, the IRS expects most new businesses to lose money during the first three years of operations. With this in mind, a new business may want to choose to operate with a business structure that will allow them to pass-through business losses so that the losses can be deducted from personal income. Basically, by choosing any type of structure other than a C corporation, the business owner may reduce their personal taxable income by the amount of the business' losses. For example, if a business owner has a family personal income of $100,000 and has business losses of $20,000, then the family will only have to pay taxes on $80,000 for that year. This could be worth over $1,000 in tax savings for the family.

In the above scenario, it would be best if the business owner chose to form an S corporation rather than a C corporation to start the business.

Keep in mind that there are procedures that will allow an S corporation to change to a C corporation later in the business's life.

The Tax Cuts and Jobs Act that was passed in December of 2017 will have a great impact on taxes paid by business owners in 2018. These changes will effect C corporations, as well as business structures that are "pass-through" entities (sole proprietorships, partnerships, LLCs and S corporations).

For C corporations, the corporate tax rate is now set permanently at 21% for all corporations regardless of the amount of income. Prior to this tax reduction, the United States had the fourth highest corporate income tax in the world, 38.91%. The only countries that had a higher tax rate at the time were the United Arab Emirates, Comoros, and Puerto Rico. Additionally, the new tax law did away with the Alternative Minimum Corporate Tax. The bottom line is that all businesses that pay a corporate income tax in the United States will pay 21% on business income.

The Tax Cuts and Jobs Act of 2017 also helped businesses that use the "pass-through" treatment of taxes. By choosing a business structure that is a "pass-through" entity, the business owner can deduct 20% of their qualified business income. Qualified business income is the "bottom line" profits of the business (business revenues less business expenses). The law does impose caps to the amount of taxable income in order to take advantage of the 20% deduction. The cap or ceiling for a single person falls on an individual earning of more than $157,500 or a married couple filing jointly earning more than $315,500. This "pass-through" provision is not currently permanent and is set to expire in the year 2025.

Bottom Line: Basically, as long as your taxable income is less than $157,500 if you are single or $315,500 if married and filing jointly, then you can deduct 20% of the business' income no matter the type of business you are in. About 70% of small businesses in the United States make less than these amounts. If your taxable income is above these amounts ($157,500 or $315,500), you will have to take a partial deduction and involves an number of calculations. Keep in mind that the

20% deduction for "pass-through" entities is set to expire in 2025. No matter your situation, it is important to talk with a tax professional to determine your exact deductions.

Is it possible to save money as a C corporation with the new tax laws?

The new corporate tax rate of 21% along with the qualified dividend tax rate of 15% for individuals makes for an interesting discussion. This conversation should start with defining what a qualified dividend is and then determine if the tax breaks can lower the tax burden of business owners.

In order to take advantage of the 15% qualified dividend tax rate, the dividend must be qualified. The dividend becomes qualified when the money comes from previously taxed profits. Therefore, the money paid out in dividends must be first taxed at the corporate income tax rate of 21%. There is even better news for those in lower income tax brackets because the qualified dividend tax rate falls to 0%. Of course with every bit of good news there is bad news. Those in earning higher income will be taxed at 20% for qualified dividends. Below is a breakdown of income and the associated qualified dividend tax rate for 2018. You should check each year for income requirements and changes to qualified dividend tax rate because they are subject to the whims of congress.

Qualified Dividend Tax Rate	Single Filers Taxable Income	Joint Filers Taxable Income	Filing as Head of Household Taxable Income
0%	$0 - $38,600	$0 - $77,200	$0 - $51,000
15%	$38,601 - $425,800	$77,201 - $479,000	$51,701 - $452,400
20%	> $425,800	> $479,000	> $452,400

When choosing a business structure, you should compare where your individual tax rate falls using a "pass-through" entity, taking into consideration the 20% "pass-through deduction, with the combination of the 21% corporation tax rate added to the qualified dividend tax rate. On

51

the following page is a breakdown of individual tax rate for 2018. Again, you should check the individual tax rates each year because they too are subject to the whims of congress.

Tax Bracket	Single Filers Tax Rate	Joint Filers Tax Rate	Head of Household Tax Rate
10%	$0 - $9,525	$0 - $19,050	$0 - $13,600
12%	$9,526 - $38,700	$19,051 - $77,400	$13,601 - $51,800
22%	$38,701 - $82,500	$77,401 - $165,000	$51,801 - $82,500
24%	$82,501 - $157,000	$165,001 - $315,000	$82,501 - $157,500
32%	$157,501 - $200,000	$315,001 - $400,000	$157,501 - $200,000
35%	$200,001 - $500,000	$400,001 - $600,000	$200,001 - $500,000
37%	> $500,000	> $600,000	>500,000

It is difficult to come up with a scenario where a business owner will overcome the double taxation of a C corporation, especially with the 20% "pass-through" deduction. For example, a single person that earns $150,000 in profit from a business and takes a 100% payout in dividends, will pay a total of $54,500 in taxes as a C corporation ($31,000 in corporate taxes and $22,500 in qualified dividend taxes). The calculation is below.

Corporate Taxes   Qualified Dividend Tax   Total Taxes Paid
$31,500 ($150,000 X .21) + $22,500 ($150,000 X .15) = $54,500

This compares to approximately $20,210 paid in taxes as an individual using the "pass-through" advantage of an S corporation. This calculation includes the 20% "pass-through" deduction and the 2018 individual tax rates. Keep in mind the owner was able to deduct 20% of the $150,000 of profit, which will allow the owner to only pay taxes on $120,000 of income.

The only time a tax advantage will occur for a C corporation is if the owner wishes to keep much of the earnings in order to grow the corporation and the owner's individual taxable income is over $200,000 if filing single. Every situation is different based on company goals and income level. It is suggested to consult with your professional tax preparer or accountant to help with your decision.

The following is a scenario of a company that has a goal of long-term growth by comparing taxes paid as a C corporation to taxes paid as an S corporation. The scenario is as follows: a business earns $500,000 in profit and the business owner wants to keep half of the earnings in the business in order to grow the business and distribute the other half of the earnings in the form of a qualified dividend to the owner as a C corporation. The C corporation must pay a 21% tax rate on the entire $500,000 ($500,000 x 21% = $105,000) and the owner must pay 15% on the $250,000 qualified dividend ($250,000 x 15% = $37,500). Keep in mind the remaining $250,000 in earnings will remain in the business for growth and will not be taxed further. The total taxes paid by the C corporation will be $142,500 ($105,000 + $37,500 = $142,500).

If the business was an S corporation in the same scenario, the entire $500,000 of profits would be taxed at the individual tax rate, due being a pass-through entity, even though $250,000 remained in the company for growth. First of all the business owner would not qualify for the 20% pass-through deduction because his income would be too high. Using the 2018 tax code, which takes into account the Tax Cuts and Jobs Act of 2017, the business owner would pay $149,189.50 in taxes if taxed as an individual on the $500,000 of business profit. As a pass-through entity, the business owner must pay taxes on the entire amount of profits even if the business leaves some of the earnings in the business for growth.

As proven in this example, if the business owner wants to leave money in the corporation for growth, then it can save money on taxes by creating a

C corporation rather than creating a pass-through entity. It is important to understand your business' long-term goals and potential for profits when choosing your business structure.

Bottom Line: It is best to choose a "pass-through" business structure early in the life of the business, especially to take advantage of business losses. Additionally, a "pass-through" entity can take advantage of the 20% deduction once the business starts making profits. Once the business starts making large profits and the owner wants to grow the business using these profits, it may make more sense to change to a C corporation. The business owner should be aware that the 20% "pass-through" deduction ends in 2025 and that tax code changes are always at the whims of congress. Therefore, it is important to stay abreast of any tax code changes, so that you can take advantage of your chosen business structure's tax treatment.

Appendix A - Quick Reference Guide To Choose Legal Business Structure

Criteria	Unincorporated Structures				Incorporated Structures		
	SP	GP	LP	LLP	LLC	S Corp	C Corp
Ownership Rules	One owner	Unlimited	Unlimited	Unlimited	Unlimited Members	Up to 75 shareholders	Unlimited
Liability Protection	Unlimited Liability	All partners have unlimited liability	Unlimited liability for general partners. Limited liability for limited partners	Limited liability for all partners	Limited liability for all members	Limited liability for all stockholders	Limited liability for all stockholders
Tax Treatment	Entity is not taxed at all. Income and losses passed through to owners.	Entity is not taxed at all. Income and losses passed through to all partners.	Entity is not taxed at all. Income and losses passed through to all partners.	Entity is not taxed at all. Income and losses passed through to all partners.	Entity is not taxed at all. Income and losses passed through to all members.	Entity is not taxed at all. Income and losses passed through to all stockholders.	Corporation is taxed at corporate tax rate. Shareholders are taxed on dividends received.
Control and Management	Sole proprietor has complete control over business.	General partners have equal say unless otherwise decided.	General partner makes decisions subject to limited partnership agreement.	The limited liability partners make decisions based on limited liability partnership agreement.	The operating agreement describes how business will be managed.	Board of directors has overall management responsibility with officers having day to day responsibility.	Board of directors has overall management responsibility with officers having day to day responsibility.
Capital Contributions	Sole proprietor makes all capital contributions as needed.	General partners contribute capital per agreement.	Both general partner and limited partner makes capital contributions per agreement.	Limited partners make capital contributions per agreement.	Members make capital contributions per agreement.	Shareholders buy stock in corporation.	Shareholders buy stock in corporation.
Perpetuity of Existence	Business dies when owner dies.	Business survives death of partner based on general partnership agreement.	Business survives death of partner based on limited partnership agreement.	Business survives death of partner based on limited liability partnership agreement.	Has perpetual existence.	Has perpetual existence.	Has perpetual existence.
Ease of Establishing	Easiest	No filing but partnership agreement needed.	File an application with secretary of state.	File an application with secretary of state.	File Articles of Organization with secretary of state.	File Articles of Incorporation with the secretary of state.	File Articles of Incorporation with the secretary of state.

SP – Sole Proprietorship
GP – General Partnership
LP – Limited Partnership
LLP – Limited Liability Partnership
LLC – Limited Liability Company
S Corp – Subchapter S Corporation
C Corp – C Corporation

Appendix B – Where to File Incorporation Forms by State

State	Website Address	Phone Number
Alabama	https://sos.alabama.gov/business-entities/domestic-corporations	334-242-7200
Alaska	https://www.commerce.alaska.gov/web/cbpl/corporations.aspx	907-269-8160
Arizona	http://www.azcc.gov/	602-542-3026
Arkansas	https://www.sos.arkansas.gov/	501-682-1010
California	http://www.sos.ca.gov/business-programs/business-entities/	916-653-6814
Colorado	http://www.sos.state.co.us/pubs/business/businessHome.html	303-894-2200
Connecticut	http://portal.ct.gov/SOTS/Common-Elements/V5-Template---Redesign/Business-Services---Home-Page	860-509-6200
Delaware	https://corp.delaware.gov/	302-739-3073
Florida	http://dos.myflorida.com/sunbiz/	850-245-6000
Georgia	https://ecorp.sos.ga.gov/	404-656-2817
Hawaii	http://cca.hawaii.gov/breg/online/	808-586-2727
Idaho	https://sos.idaho.gov/	208-334-2301
Illinois	https://www2.illinois.gov/business/manage-your-business/SOS/llc-filings	217-782-6961
Indiana	https://www.in.gov/sos/business/	317-232-6576
Iowa	https://sos.iowa.gov/	888-767-8683
Kansas	http://www.kcc.state.ks.us/	785-271-3100
Kentucky	https://www.sos.ky.gov/bus/businessfilings/OnlineServices/Pages/default.aspx	502-564-3490
Louisiana	https://www.sos.la.gov/Pages/default.aspx	225-922-2880
Maine	http://www.maine.gov/sos/cec/corp/	207-626-8400
Maryland	http://dat.maryland.gov/businesses/pages/default.aspx	410-767-1184
Massachusetts	https://www.sec.state.ma.us/cor/	617-727-9640
Michigan	https://www.michigan.gov/lara/0,4601,7-154-61343_35413---,00.html	517-373-1820
Minnesota	https://www.sos.state.mn.us/business-liens	651-296-2803
Mississippi	http://www.sos.ms.gov/BusinessServices/Pages/default.aspx	601-359-1633
Missouri	https://www.sos.mo.gov/business/corporations	573-751-4153
Montana	http://sos.mt.gov/business	406-444-3665
Nebraska	http://www.sos.ne.gov/business/corp_serv/	402-471-4079
Nevada	https://nvsos.gov/sos/businesses	775-684-5708
New Hampshire	http://sos.nh.gov/corp_div.aspx	603-271-3242
New Jersey	http://www.nj.gov/treasury/revenue/filecerts.shtml	609-292-6748
New Mexico	http://www.sos.state.nm.us/Business_Services/Corporations_Overview.aspx	505-827-3614
New York	https://www.dos.ny.gov/corps/	518-473-2492
North Carolina	https://www.sosnc.gov/divisions/business_registration	919-814-5400
North Dakota	https://sos.nd.gov/business/business-services	701-328-2900
Ohio	https://www.sos.state.oh.us/businesses/#gref	614-466-2655
Oklahoma	https://www.sos.ok.gov/business/default.aspx	405-522-2520
Oregon	http://sos.oregon.gov/business/Pages/default.aspx	503-986-2200
Pennsylvania	http://www.dos.pa.gov/BusinessCharities/Business/Pages/default.aspx	717-787-1057
Rhode Island	http://sos.ri.gov/divisions/business-portal	401-222-3040
South Carolina	http://www.sos.sc.gov/BusinessFilings	803-734-2158
Tennessee	https://tnbear.tn.gov/ecommerce/default.aspx	615-741-2286
Texas	https://www.sos.state.tx.us/corp/index.shtml	512-463-5555
Utah	https://corporations.utah.gov/	801-530-4849
Vermont	https://www.sec.state.vt.us/corporationsbusiness-services.aspx	802-828-2363
Virginia	http://www.scc.virginia.gov/	804-371-9733
Washington	https://www.sos.wa.gov/corps/	360-725-0377
West Virginia	https://sos.wv.gov/business-licensing/business/Pages/businessdivision.aspx	304-558-8000
Wisconsin	https://www.wdfi.org/corporations/	608-261-7577
Wyoming	http://soswy.state.wy.us/Business/Default.aspx	307-777-7311
Washington DC	https://dcra.dc.gov/business-licensing-online-services	202-442-4400

Appendix C – Example Articles of Organization for a Virginia LLC

*Every state has different requirements and templates – check with your state.

Form
LLC-1011

(Rev. 12/2017)

Virginia State
Corporation
Commission

**Articles of Organization
Virginia Limited Liability Company**

▶ See instructions that follow

Print Form

**Filing Fee:
$100.00**

Pursuant to Chapter 12 of Title 13.1 of the Code of Virginia the undersigned states as follows:

Article I

The name of the limited liability company ("the company") is:

The Golf Shop LLC

(The name must contain the words **limited company** or **limited liability company** or the abbreviation **L.C., LC, L.L.C. or LLC**)

Article II

A. The name of the company's initial registered agent is:

John D Smith

B. The initial registered agent is (mark appropriate box):

(1) an INDIVIDUAL who is a resident of Virginia **and**
☑ a member or manager of the limited liability company.
☐ a member or manager of a limited liability company that is a member or manager of the limited liability company.
☐ an officer or director of a corporation that is a member or manager of the limited liability company.
☐ a general partner of a general or limited partnership that is a member or manager of the limited liability company.
☐ a trustee of a trust that is a member or manager of the limited liability company.
☐ a member of the Virginia State Bar.

OR

(2) ☐ a domestic or foreign stock or nonstock corporation, limited liability company or registered limited liability partnership authorized to transact business in Virginia.

Article III

A. The company's initial registered office address, including the street and number, if any, which is identical to the business office of the initial registered agent, is:

125 North Main Street   Richmond   VA 24111
(number/street)   (city or town)   (zip)

B. The registered office is located in the ☐ county or ☑ city of: Richmond

Article IV

The company's principal office address, including the street and number, is:

125 North Main Street   Richmond   VA   24111
(number/street)   (city or town)   (state)   (zip)

Signature(s) of Organizer(s):

Signature	Printed Name	Date	Telephone No. (optional)
	John D Smith	1/18/18	555-555-5555
	Bob B Smith	1/18/18	555-555-5554

Articles of Organization Instructions

Filing Requirements	
Include filing fee of $100.00	
Paper Filing	**Online Filing**
Download from www.scc.virginia.gov/clk/dom_llc.aspx, complete, print, and mail to below address.	Visit https://sccefile.scc.virginia.gov/NewEntity to complete and file in real time or to submit a PDF
Include a check payable to State Corporation Commission. **DO NOT SEND CASH.**	Pay online with a credit card.

Specific Instructions

Article I Name

The proposed name must be distinguishable from other entity names on record with the Commission. To check the availability of a name, visit our website, https://sccefile.scc.virginia.gov/NameAvailability, or contact the Clerk's Office.

Article II Registered Agent

The registered agent's sole duty is to receive legal documents and notices on behalf of the entity. The limited liability company may not serve as its own registered agent. The registered agent must be an individual or entity that meets one of the qualifications, check the applicable box.

Article III Registered Office Address

The registered office location must be identical to the registered agent's business office.

    Only use a rural route and box number if:
- The registered office's location has no street address.

    Only use a post office box if
- There is no street address or rural route and box number.
- The town/city has a population of 2,000 or less.

Provide the name of the county or independent city where the registered office is located.

Article IV Principal Office Address

The principal office is the location of the company's principal executive offices. The company must keep a current list of its members and other internal company records at the principal office. Only use a rural route and box number if a principal office has no street address. A post office box is not allowed.

Signature(s) of Organizer(s)

One or more organizers must sign the articles. Include the signature and printed name of each person who signs.

If signing on behalf of an organizer that is a business entity, include the business entity's name, your printed name, and your role within the business entity.

Questions? Call (804) 371-9733 or 1-866-722-2551 (toll-free in Virginia)

Where To Submit Paper Documents	
Mailing Address:	Counter Delivery Address:
State Corporation Commission	State Corporation Commission
Clerk's Office	Clerk's Office, First Floor
PO Box 1197	1300 E. Main St.
Richmond, VA 23218-1197	Richmond, VA 23219

Important Information

This form contains the minimum Virginia requirements for articles of organization. If the articles of organization needs to include additional provisions, **separately** prepare and submit typewritten articles of organization that cover the minimum requirements, using the following guidelines:
- size 8 1/2" x 11"
- one-sided
- no visible watermarks or background logos
- minimum 1" margin on all sides

Form **LLC-1011** (Rev. 12/2017)

Appendix D – Example Articles of Incorporation for a Virginia Corporation

*Every state has different requirements and templates – check with your state.

COMMONWEALTH OF VIRGINIA
STATE CORPORATION COMMISSION

SCC644
(07/06)

ARTICLES OF INCORPORATION
OF A VIRGINIA PROFESSIONAL STOCK CORPORATION

The undersigned, pursuant to Chapters 7 and 9 of Title 13.1 of the Code of Virginia, state(s) as follows:

1. The name of the professional corporation is

   The Golf Shop Inc.

2. The professional corporation is organized for the sole and specific purpose of rendering the professional

   services of ___Retail sales of golf equipment___.

3. The number of shares authorized to be issued by the corporation is ___100,000___.

4. A. The name of the professional corporation's initial registered agent is

   ___John D. Smith___.

   B. The initial registered agent is (mark appropriate box):
      (1) an individual who is a resident of Virginia and

      X an initial director of the professional corporation.
      ☐ a member of the Virginia State Bar.
         OR
      (2) ☐ a domestic or foreign stock or nonstock corporation, limited liability company, or registered
          limited liability partnership authorized to transact business in Virginia.

5. A. The professional corporation's initial registered office address, including the street and number, if any,
      which is identical to the business office of the initial registered agent, is

   ___155 North Main St___   ___Richmond___, VA ___24111___
        (number/street)   (city or town)   (zip)

   B. The registered office is physically located in the ☐ county or X city of ___Richmond___.

6. The first board of directors shall have ___2___ member(s).

7. The initial directors are:

   NAME(S)   ADDRESS(ES)

   ___John D. Smith___   ___455 South Main St.___
                                    ___Richmond VA 24111___

   ___Bob B Smith___   ___455 South Main St.___
                                    ___Richmond VA 24111___

8. The undersigned INCORPORATOR(s) is (are) duly licensed or legally authorized to render the listed
   professional services, and at least one incorporator is so licensed or legally authorized in Virginia.

   _____   ___John D Smith___

   _____   ___Bob B Smith___
        SIGNATURE(S)   PRINTED NAME(S)

   Telephone number (optional): _____

See instructions on the reverse.

NOTES

The articles must be in the English language, typewritten or printed in black, legible and reproducible.

This form contains the minimum number of provisions required by Virginia law to be set forth in the articles of incorporation of a professional stock corporation. If additional provisions are desired, then the complete articles of incorporation, including the additional provisions, must be typewritten or printed on white, opaque paper 8 1/2" by 11" in size, using only one side of a page, and free of visible watermarks and background logos. A minimum of a 1" margin must be provided on the left, top and bottom margins of a page and 1/2" at the right margin. This form may not be submitted with an attachment.

You can download this form from our website at www.scc.virginia.gov/clk/formfee.aspx

INSTRUCTIONS

1. **Name:** The corporate name must contain the word "corporation," "incorporated," "company" or "limited"; or the abbreviation "corp.," "inc.," "co." or "ltd."; or the initials "P.C.," or "PC"; or the phrase "professional corporation" or "a professional corporation" at the end of its corporate name. The proposed name must be distinguishable upon the records of the Commission. See §§ 13.1-544.1 and 13.1-630 of the Code of Virginia. To check the availability of a corporate name, please contact the Clerk's Office Call Center at (804) 371-9733 or toll-free in Virginia at (866) 722-2551.

2. **Professional services:** State the professional services the corporation is organized to render. The law limits such services to the personal services rendered by: pharmacists, optometrists, practitioners of the healing arts, nurse practitioners, practitioners of the behavioral science professions, veterinarians, surgeons, dentists, architects, professional engineers, land surveyors, certified interior designers, certified landscape architects, public accountants, certified public accountants, attorneys-at-law, insurance consultants, audiologists or speech pathologists and clinical nurse specialists. See § 13.1-543 of the Code of Virginia.

3. **Shares:** If a stock corporation, list the total number of shares the corporation is authorized to issue issue (note: the charter fee and annual registration fee are based on the number of authorized shares). If more than one class or series of shares is to be authorized, the articles must set forth the number of authorized shares of each class or series and a distinguishing designation for each class or series (e.g., common, preferred, etc.) and set forth the preferences, rights and limitations of each class or series. See §§ 13.1-619 and 13.1-638 of the Code of Virginia. For the percentage of shareholders that must be licensed or authorized to render the same services for which the corporation is organized, see §§ 13.1-549 and 13.1-549.1 of the Code of Virginia.

4. **Registered agent:** A. Provide the name of the registered agent. The corporation may not serve as its own registered agent. See §§ 13.1-619 and 13.1-634 of the Code of Virginia.
    B. Check one of the boxes to indicate the qualification of the registered agent. The registered agent must be one of the options listed. No other person or entity may serve as the registered agent.

5. **Registered office:** A. The location of the registered office must be identical to the business office of the registered agent. See § 13.1-634 of the Code of Virginia. The address of the registered office must include a street address. A rural route and box number may only be used if no street address is associated with the registered office's location. A post office box is only acceptable for towns/cities that have a population of 2,000 or less if no street address or rural route and box number is associated with the registered office's location.
    B. Provide the name of the county or independent city where the registered office is physically located. Counties and independent cities in Virginia are separate local jurisdictions. See §§ 13.1-619 and 13.1-634 of the Code of Virginia.

6&7. **Directors:** The articles must fix the number of the corporation's first board of directors. A corporation can have directors immediately upon formation only if they are named in the articles. Thus, if the registered agent's qualification in 4.B is that of an initial director, then all the initial directors must be included. NOTE: The licensing restriction on shareholders referenced above in Instruction 3, also applies to directors. See § 13.1-553 of the Code of Virginia.

8. **Incorporator(s):** One or more persons must sign the articles in this capacity; all incorporators must be licensed or authorized to render the listed professional services, and at least one incorporator must be licensed or authorized to render the professional services in Virginia. See §§ 13.1-544 and 13.1-604 of the Code of Virginia.

It is a Class 1 misdemeanor for any person to sign a document he or she knows is false in any material respect with intent that the document be delivered to the Commission for filing.

Submit the original, signed articles to the Clerk of the State Corporation Commission, P. O. Box 1197, Richmond, Virginia 23218-1197, (Street address: 1300 E. Main Street, Tyler Building, 1st floor, Richmond, Virginia 23219), along with a check for the charter and filing fees for the total amount, payable to the State Corporation Commission. PLEASE DO NOT SEND CASH. If you have any questions, please call (804) 371-9733 or toll-free in Virginia, 1-888-722-2661.

Charter fee: 1,000,000 or fewer authorized shares - $50 for each 25,000 shares or fraction thereof; more than 1 million shares - $2,500. Filing fee: $25.

Acknowledgements

As an entrepreneur and an educator, I am always interested on how to protect personal wealth and save on taxes. These two items are key ingredients to consider when choosing a legal business structure. When congress passed the Tax Cuts and Jobs Act in December of 2017, it caused me to once again investigate the importance of choosing the right legal business structure of a business.

My students' questions about the impact of this Act on businesses caused me to research the impact on businesses and inspired me to write this book. I hope that it will help new entrepreneurs and existing business owners to think about their goals and tax situation in order to choose the right business structure for the business.

As always, I dedicate this book to my wife, Lavon, and daughter, Faron, who continue to support all of my endeavors.